Mileage Logbook

Name:	Position:
Adress:	
Mobile:	
Telephone:	
Email:	
Fax:	

Book info :

Book No.:	
Start Date:	End Date:

Notes:

_____

_____

_____

_____

_____

_____

Vehicle Mileage Logbook

						Sheet no.:		

Make :		Model :		Year :		License number :		

DATE	PURPOSE OF TRAVEL	JOURNEY		ODOMETER READING			TOTAL MILES	
		From	To	Start	End	Distance (km)	Business	Private

Daily checks	Tires/ Wheel	Wipers	Lights	Mirrors	Horn	Seatbelts	Brakes	Coupling devices
Monday								
Tuesday								
Wednesday								
Thursday								
Friday								
Saturday								
Sunday								

Fuel Input				
Date	Quantity	Unit	Mileage	Units

Notes :
_____
_____
_____
_____
_____
_____
_____
_____

Signature :

Vehicle Mileage Logbook

Sheet no.:

Make : **Model :** **Year :** **License number :**

DATE	PURPOSE OF TRAVEL	JOURNEY		ODOMETER READING			TOTAL MILES	
		From	To	Start	End	Distance (km)	Business	Private

Daily checks	Tires/ Wheel	Wipers	Lights	Mirrors	Horn	Seatbelts	Brakes	Coupling devices
Monday								
Tuesday								
Wednesday								
Thursday								
Friday								
Saturday								
Sunday								

Fuel Input

Date	Quantity	Unit	Mileage	Units

Notes :

_____
_____
_____
_____
_____
_____
_____
_____

Signature :

Vehicle Mileage Logbook

Sheet no.:

Make :   Model :   Year :   License number :

DATE	PURPOSE OF TRAVEL	JOURNEY		ODOMETER READING			TOTAL MILES	
		From	To	Start	End	Distance (km)	Business	Private

Daily checks	Tires/ Wheel	Wipers	Lights	Mirrors	Horn	Seatbelts	Brakes	Coupling devices
Monday								
Tuesday								
Wednesday								
Thursday								
Friday								
Saturday								
Sunday								

Fuel Input				
Date	Quantity	Unit	Mileage	Units

Notes :

_____
_____
_____
_____
_____
_____
_____
_____

Signature :

Vehicle Mileage Logbook

Sheet no.:

Make :   Model :   Year :   License number :

DATE	PURPOSE OF TRAVEL	JOURNEY		ODOMETER READING			TOTAL MILES	
		From	To	Start	End	Distance (km)	Business	Private

Daily checks	Tires/ Wheel	Wipers	Lights	Mirrors	Horn	Seatbelts	Brakes	Coupling devices
Monday								
Tuesday								
Wednesday								
Thursday								
Friday								
Saturday								
Sunday								

Fuel Input				
Date	Quantity	Unit	Mileage	Units

Notes :

Signature :

Vehicle Mileage Logbook

Sheet no.:

Make :   Model :   Year :   License number :

DATE	PURPOSE OF TRAVEL	JOURNEY		ODOMETER READING			TOTAL MILES	
		From	To	Start	End	Distance (km)	Business	Private

Daily checks	Tires/ Wheel	Wipers	Lights	Mirrors	Horn	Seatbelts	Brakes	Coupling devices
Monday								
Tuesday								
Wednesday								
Thursday								
Friday								
Saturday								
Sunday								

Fuel Input				
Date	Quantity	Unit	Mileage	Units

Notes :

Signature :

Vehicle Mileage Logbook

Sheet no.:

Make :   Model :   Year :   License number :

DATE	PURPOSE OF TRAVEL	JOURNEY		ODOMETER READING			TOTAL MILES	
		From	To	Start	End	Distance (km)	Business	Private

Daily checks	Tires/ Wheel	Wipers	Lights	Mirrors	Horn	Seatbelts	Brakes	Coupling devices
Monday								
Tuesday								
Wednesday								
Thursday								
Friday								
Saturday								
Sunday								

Fuel Input				
Date	Quantity	Unit	Mileage	Units

Notes :

Signature :

Vehicle Mileage Logbook

Sheet no.:

Make :   Model :   Year :   License number :

DATE	PURPOSE OF TRAVEL	JOURNEY		ODOMETER READING			TOTAL MILES	
		From	To	Start	End	Distance (km)	Business	Private

Daily checks	Tires/ Wheel	Wipers	Lights	Mirrors	Horn	Seatbelts	Brakes	Coupling devices
Monday								
Tuesday								
Wednesday								
Thursday								
Friday								
Saturday								
Sunday								

Fuel Input				
Date	Quantity	Unit	Mileage	Units

Notes :

_____
_____
_____
_____
_____
_____
_____
_____
_____

Signature :

Vehicle Mileage Logbook

Sheet no.:

Make :   Model :   Year :   License number :

DATE	PURPOSE OF TRAVEL	JOURNEY		ODOMETER READING			TOTAL MILES	
		From	To	Start	End	Distance (km)	Business	Private

Daily checks	Tires/ Wheel	Wipers	Lights	Mirrors	Horn	Seatbelts	Brakes	Coupling devices
Monday								
Tuesday								
Wednesday								
Thursday								
Friday								
Saturday								
Sunday								

Fuel Input				
Date	Quantity	Unit	Mileage	Units

Notes :

_____
_____
_____
_____
_____
_____
_____

Signature :

Vehicle Mileage Logbook

Sheet no.:

Make :   Model :   Year :   License number :

DATE	PURPOSE OF TRAVEL	JOURNEY		ODOMETER READING			TOTAL MILES	
		From	To	Start	End	Distance (km)	Business	Private

Daily checks	Tires/ Wheel	Wipers	Lights	Mirrors	Horn	Seatbelts	Brakes	Coupling devices
Monday								
Tuesday								
Wednesday								
Thursday								
Friday								
Saturday								
Sunday								

Fuel Input				
Date	Quantity	Unit	Mileage	Units

Notes :

_____
_____
_____
_____
_____
_____
_____

Signature :

Vehicle Mileage Logbook

Sheet no.:

Make :   Model :   Year :   License number :

DATE	PURPOSE OF TRAVEL	JOURNEY		ODOMETER READING			TOTAL MILES	
		From	To	Start	End	Distance (km)	Business	Private

Daily checks	Tires/ Wheel	Wipers	Lights	Mirrors	Horn	Seatbelts	Brakes	Coupling devices
Monday								
Tuesday								
Wednesday								
Thursday								
Friday								
Saturday								
Sunday								

Fuel Input				
Date	Quantity	Unit	Mileage	Units

Notes :

_____

_____

_____

_____

_____

_____

_____

Signature :

Vehicle Mileage Logbook

Sheet no.:

Make :   Model :   Year :   License number :

DATE	PURPOSE OF TRAVEL	JOURNEY		ODOMETER READING			TOTAL MILES	
		From	To	Start	End	Distance (km)	Business	Private

Daily checks	Tires/ Wheel	Wipers	Lights	Mirrors	Horn	Seatbelts	Brakes	Coupling devices
Monday								
Tuesday								
Wednesday								
Thursday								
Friday								
Saturday								
Sunday								

Fuel Input				
Date	Quantity	Unit	Mileage	Units

Notes :

_____
_____
_____
_____
_____
_____
_____
_____

Signature :

Vehicle Mileage Logbook

Sheet no.:

Make :   Model :   Year :   License number :

DATE	PURPOSE OF TRAVEL	JOURNEY		ODOMETER READING			TOTAL MILES	
		From	To	Start	End	Distance (km)	Business	Private

Daily checks	Tires/ Wheel	Wipers	Lights	Mirrors	Horn	Seatbelts	Brakes	Coupling devices
Monday								
Tuesday								
Wednesday								
Thursday								
Friday								
Saturday								
Sunday								

Fuel Input				
Date	Quantity	Unit	Mileage	Units

Notes :

_____

_____

_____

_____

_____

_____

_____

Signature :

Vehicle Mileage Logbook

Sheet no.:

Make :   Model :   Year :   License number :

DATE	PURPOSE OF TRAVEL	JOURNEY		ODOMETER READING			TOTAL MILES	
		From	To	Start	End	Distance (km)	Business	Private

Daily checks	Tires/ Wheel	Wipers	Lights	Mirrors	Horn	Seatbelts	Brakes	Coupling devices
Monday								
Tuesday								
Wednesday								
Thursday								
Friday								
Saturday								
Sunday								

Fuel Input				
Date	Quantity	Unit	Mileage	Units

Notes :

Signature :

Vehicle Mileage Logbook

Sheet no.:

Make : Model : Year : License number :

DATE	PURPOSE OF TRAVEL	JOURNEY		ODOMETER READING			TOTAL MILES	
		From	To	Start	End	Distance (km)	Business	Private

Daily checks	Tires/ Wheel	Wipers	Lights	Mirrors	Horn	Seatbelts	Brakes	Coupling devices
Monday								
Tuesday								
Wednesday								
Thursday								
Friday								
Saturday								
Sunday								

Fuel Input				
Date	Quantity	Unit	Mileage	Units

Notes :

Signature :

Vehicle Mileage Logbook

Sheet no.:

Make :   Model :   Year :   License number :

DATE	PURPOSE OF TRAVEL	JOURNEY		ODOMETER READING			TOTAL MILES	
		From	To	Start	End	Distance (km)	Business	Private

Daily checks	Tires/ Wheel	Wipers	Lights	Mirrors	Horn	Seatbelts	Brakes	Coupling devices
Monday								
Tuesday								
Wednesday								
Thursday								
Friday								
Saturday								
Sunday								

Fuel Input				
Date	Quantity	Unit	Mileage	Units

Notes :

_____
_____
_____
_____
_____
_____
_____
_____

Signature :

Vehicle Mileage Logbook

Sheet no.:

Make :   Model :   Year :   License number :

DATE	PURPOSE OF TRAVEL	JOURNEY		ODOMETER READING			TOTAL MILES	
		From	To	Start	End	Distance (km)	Business	Private

Daily checks	Tires/ Wheel	Wipers	Lights	Mirrors	Horn	Seatbelts	Brakes	Coupling devices
Monday								
Tuesday								
Wednesday								
Thursday								
Friday								
Saturday								
Sunday								

Fuel Input				
Date	Quantity	Unit	Mileage	Units

Notes :

_____
_____
_____
_____
_____
_____
_____
_____

Signature :

Vehicle Mileage Logbook

Sheet no.:

Make : | Model : | Year : | License number :

DATE	PURPOSE OF TRAVEL	JOURNEY		ODOMETER READING			TOTAL MILES	
		From	To	Start	End	Distance (km)	Business	Private

Daily checks	Tires/ Wheel	Wipers	Lights	Mirrors	Horn	Seatbelts	Brakes	Coupling devices
Monday								
Tuesday								
Wednesday								
Thursday								
Friday								
Saturday								
Sunday								

Fuel Input				
Date	Quantity	Unit	Mileage	Units

Notes :

_____
_____
_____
_____
_____
_____
_____
_____

Signature :

Vehicle Mileage Logbook

Sheet no.:

Make :　　　Model :　　　Year :　　License number :

DATE	PURPOSE OF TRAVEL	JOURNEY		ODOMETER READING			TOTAL MILES	
		From	To	Start	End	Distance (km)	Business	Private

Daily checks	Tires/ Wheel	Wipers	Lights	Mirrors	Horn	Seatbelts	Brakes	Coupling devices
Monday								
Tuesday								
Wednesday								
Thursday								
Friday								
Saturday								
Sunday								

Fuel Input				
Date	Quantity	Unit	Mileage	Units

Notes :

_____
_____
_____
_____
_____
_____
_____

Signature :

Vehicle Mileage Logbook

Sheet no.:

Make :   Model :   Year :   License number :

DATE	PURPOSE OF TRAVEL	JOURNEY		ODOMETER READING			TOTAL MILES	
		From	To	Start	End	Distance (km)	Business	Private

Daily checks	Tires/ Wheel	Wipers	Lights	Mirrors	Horn	Seatbelts	Brakes	Coupling devices
Monday								
Tuesday								
Wednesday								
Thursday								
Friday								
Saturday								
Sunday								

Fuel Input				
Date	Quantity	Unit	Mileage	Units

Notes :

Signature :

Vehicle Mileage Logbook

Sheet no.:

Make :   **Model :**   **Year :**   **License number :**

DATE	PURPOSE OF TRAVEL	JOURNEY		ODOMETER READING			TOTAL MILES	
		From	To	Start	End	Distance (km)	Business	Private

Daily checks	Tires/ Wheel	Wipers	Lights	Mirrors	Horn	Seatbelts	Brakes	Coupling devices
Monday								
Tuesday								
Wednesday								
Thursday								
Friday								
Saturday								
Sunday								

Fuel Input				
Date	Quantity	Unit	Mileage	Units

Notes :

_____

_____

_____

_____

_____

_____

_____

Signature :

Vehicle Mileage Logbook

Sheet no.:

Make :   Model :   Year :   License number :

DATE	PURPOSE OF TRAVEL	JOURNEY		ODOMETER READING			TOTAL MILES	
		From	To	Start	End	Distance (km)	Business	Private

Daily checks	Tires/ Wheel	Wipers	Lights	Mirrors	Horn	Seatbelts	Brakes	Coupling devices
Monday								
Tuesday								
Wednesday								
Thursday								
Friday								
Saturday								
Sunday								

Fuel Input				
Date	Quantity	Unit	Mileage	Units

Notes :

_____
_____
_____
_____
_____
_____
_____
_____

Signature :

Vehicle Mileage Logbook

Sheet no.:

Make :   Model :   Year :   License number :

DATE	PURPOSE OF TRAVEL	JOURNEY		ODOMETER READING			TOTAL MILES	
		From	To	Start	End	Distance (km)	Business	Private

Daily checks	Tires/ Wheel	Wipers	Lights	Mirrors	Horn	Seatbelts	Brakes	Coupling devices
Monday								
Tuesday								
Wednesday								
Thursday								
Friday								
Saturday								
Sunday								

Fuel Input				
Date	Quantity	Unit	Mileage	Units

Notes :

Signature :

Vehicle Mileage Logbook

Sheet no.:

Make :   Model :   Year :   License number :

DATE	PURPOSE OF TRAVEL	JOURNEY		ODOMETER READING			TOTAL MILES	
		From	To	Start	End	Distance (km)	Business	Private

Daily checks	Tires/ Wheel	Wipers	Lights	Mirrors	Horn	Seatbelts	Brakes	Coupling devices
Monday								
Tuesday								
Wednesday								
Thursday								
Friday								
Saturday								
Sunday								

Fuel Input				
Date	Quantity	Unit	Mileage	Units

Notes :

Signature :

Vehicle Mileage Logbook

Sheet no.:

Make :   Model :   Year :   License number :

DATE	PURPOSE OF TRAVEL	JOURNEY		ODOMETER READING			TOTAL MILES	
		From	To	Start	End	Distance (km)	Business	Private

Daily checks	Tires/ Wheel	Wipers	Lights	Mirrors	Horn	Seatbelts	Brakes	Coupling devices
Monday								
Tuesday								
Wednesday								
Thursday								
Friday								
Saturday								
Sunday								

Fuel Input				
Date	Quantity	Unit	Mileage	Units

Notes :

_____
_____
_____
_____
_____
_____
_____
_____

Signature :

Vehicle Mileage Logbook

Sheet no.:

Make :   Model :   Year :   License number :

DATE	PURPOSE OF TRAVEL	JOURNEY		ODOMETER READING			TOTAL MILES	
		From	To	Start	End	Distance (km)	Business	Private

Daily checks	Tires/ Wheel	Wipers	Lights	Mirrors	Horn	Seatbelts	Brakes	Coupling devices
Monday								
Tuesday								
Wednesday								
Thursday								
Friday								
Saturday								
Sunday								

Fuel Input				
Date	Quantity	Unit	Mileage	Units

Notes :

_____

_____

_____

_____

_____

_____

_____

Signature :

Vehicle Mileage Logbook

Sheet no.:

Make : Model : Year : License number :

DATE	PURPOSE OF TRAVEL	JOURNEY		ODOMETER READING			TOTAL MILES	
		From	To	Start	End	Distance (km)	Business	Private

Daily checks	Tires/ Wheel	Wipers	Lights	Mirrors	Horn	Seatbelts	Brakes	Coupling devices
Monday								
Tuesday								
Wednesday								
Thursday								
Friday								
Saturday								
Sunday								

Fuel Input				
Date	Quantity	Unit	Mileage	Units

Notes :

_____
_____
_____
_____
_____
_____
_____

Signature :

Vehicle Mileage Logbook

Sheet no.:

Make : Model : Year : License number :

DATE	PURPOSE OF TRAVEL	JOURNEY		ODOMETER READING			TOTAL MILES	
		From	To	Start	End	Distance (km)	Business	Private

Daily checks	Tires/ Wheel	Wipers	Lights	Mirrors	Horn	Seatbelts	Brakes	Coupling devices
Monday								
Tuesday								
Wednesday								
Thursday								
Friday								
Saturday								
Sunday								

Fuel Input				
Date	Quantity	Unit	Mileage	Units

Notes :

Signature :

Vehicle Mileage Logbook

Sheet no.:

Make : Model : Year : License number :

DATE	PURPOSE OF TRAVEL	JOURNEY		ODOMETER READING			TOTAL MILES	
		From	To	Start	End	Distance (km)	Business	Private

Daily checks	Tires/ Wheel	Wipers	Lights	Mirrors	Horn	Seatbelts	Brakes	Coupling devices
Monday								
Tuesday								
Wednesday								
Thursday								
Friday								
Saturday								
Sunday								

Fuel Input				
Date	Quantity	Unit	Mileage	Units

Notes :

_____
_____
_____
_____
_____
_____
_____
_____

Signature :

Vehicle Mileage Logbook

Sheet no.:

Make :	Model :	Year :	License number :

DATE	PURPOSE OF TRAVEL	JOURNEY		ODOMETER READING			TOTAL MILES	
		From	To	Start	End	Distance (km)	Business	Private

Daily checks	Tires/ Wheel	Wipers	Lights	Mirrors	Horn	Seatbelts	Brakes	Coupling devices
Monday								
Tuesday								
Wednesday								
Thursday								
Friday								
Saturday								
Sunday								

Fuel Input				
Date	Quantity	Unit	Mileage	Units

Notes :

Signature :

Vehicle Mileage Logbook

Sheet no.:

Make :   Model :   Year :   License number :

DATE	PURPOSE OF TRAVEL	JOURNEY		ODOMETER READING			TOTAL MILES	
		From	To	Start	End	Distance (km)	Business	Private

Daily checks	Tires/ Wheel	Wipers	Lights	Mirrors	Horn	Seatbelts	Brakes	Coupling devices
Monday								
Tuesday								
Wednesday								
Thursday								
Friday								
Saturday								
Sunday								

Fuel Input				
Date	Quantity	Unit	Mileage	Units

Notes :

_____
_____
_____
_____
_____
_____
_____

Signature :

Vehicle Mileage Logbook

Sheet no.:

Make : Model : Year : License number :

DATE	PURPOSE OF TRAVEL	JOURNEY		ODOMETER READING			TOTAL MILES	
		From	To	Start	End	Distance (km)	Business	Private

Daily checks	Tires/ Wheel	Wipers	Lights	Mirrors	Horn	Seatbelts	Brakes	Coupling devices
Monday								
Tuesday								
Wednesday								
Thursday								
Friday								
Saturday								
Sunday								

Fuel Input				
Date	Quantity	Unit	Mileage	Units

Notes :

_____

_____

_____

_____

_____

_____

_____

Signature :

Vehicle Mileage Logbook

Sheet no.:

Make :   Model :   Year :   License number :

DATE	PURPOSE OF TRAVEL	JOURNEY		ODOMETER READING			TOTAL MILES	
		From	To	Start	End	Distance (km)	Business	Private

Daily checks	Tires/ Wheel	Wipers	Lights	Mirrors	Horn	Seatbelts	Brakes	Coupling devices
Monday								
Tuesday								
Wednesday								
Thursday								
Friday								
Saturday								
Sunday								

Fuel Input				
Date	Quantity	Unit	Mileage	Units

Notes :

_____
_____
_____
_____
_____
_____
_____
_____

Signature :

Vehicle Mileage Logbook

Sheet no.:

Make :   Model :   Year :   License number :

| DATE | PURPOSE OF TRAVEL | JOURNEY | | ODOMETER READING | | | TOTAL MILES | |
		From	To	Start	End	Distance (km)	Business	Private

Daily checks	Tires/ Wheel	Wipers	Lights	Mirrors	Horn	Seatbelts	Brakes	Coupling devices
Monday								
Tuesday								
Wednesday								
Thursday								
Friday								
Saturday								
Sunday								

| Fuel Input | | | | |
Date	Quantity	Unit	Mileage	Units

Notes :

_____
_____
_____
_____
_____
_____
_____
_____
_____

Signature :

Vehicle Mileage Logbook

Sheet no.:

Make :	Model :	Year :	License number :

DATE	PURPOSE OF TRAVEL	JOURNEY		ODOMETER READING			TOTAL MILES	
		From	To	Start	End	Distance (km)	Business	Private

Daily checks	Tires/ Wheel	Wipers	Lights	Mirrors	Horn	Seatbelts	Brakes	Coupling devices
Monday								
Tuesday								
Wednesday								
Thursday								
Friday								
Saturday								
Sunday								

Fuel Input				
Date	Quantity	Unit	Mileage	Units

Notes :

_____

_____

_____

_____

_____

_____

_____

Signature :

Vehicle Mileage Logbook

Sheet no.:

Make :　　　　Model :　　　　Year :　　　License number :

DATE	PURPOSE OF TRAVEL	JOURNEY		ODOMETER READING			TOTAL MILES	
		From	To	Start	End	Distance (km)	Business	Private

Daily checks	Tires/ Wheel	Wipers	Lights	Mirrors	Horn	Seatbelts	Brakes	Coupling devices
Monday								
Tuesday								
Wednesday								
Thursday								
Friday								
Saturday								
Sunday								

Fuel Input				
Date	Quantity	Unit	Mileage	Units

Notes :

Signature :

Vehicle Mileage Logbook

Sheet no.:

Make :   Model :   Year :   License number :

DATE	PURPOSE OF TRAVEL	JOURNEY		ODOMETER READING			TOTAL MILES	
		From	To	Start	End	Distance (km)	Business	Private

Daily checks	Tires/ Wheel	Wipers	Lights	Mirrors	Horn	Seatbelts	Brakes	Coupling devices
Monday								
Tuesday								
Wednesday								
Thursday								
Friday								
Saturday								
Sunday								

Fuel Input				
Date	Quantity	Unit	Mileage	Units

Notes :

_____
_____
_____
_____
_____
_____
_____
_____
_____

Signature :

Vehicle Mileage Logbook

Sheet no.:

Make :　　　　　Model :　　　　　Year :　　　License number :

DATE	PURPOSE OF TRAVEL	JOURNEY		ODOMETER READING			TOTAL MILES	
		From	To	Start	End	Distance (km)	Business	Private

Daily checks	Tires/ Wheel	Wipers	Lights	Mirrors	Horn	Seatbelts	Brakes	Coupling devices
Monday								
Tuesday								
Wednesday								
Thursday								
Friday								
Saturday								
Sunday								

Fuel Input				
Date	Quantity	Unit	Mileage	Units

Notes :

_____

Signature :

Vehicle Mileage Logbook

Sheet no.:

Make :   Model :   Year :   License number :

DATE	PURPOSE OF TRAVEL	JOURNEY		ODOMETER READING			TOTAL MILES	
		From	To	Start	End	Distance (km)	Business	Private

Daily checks	Tires/ Wheel	Wipers	Lights	Mirrors	Horn	Seatbelts	Brakes	Coupling devices
Monday								
Tuesday								
Wednesday								
Thursday								
Friday								
Saturday								
Sunday								

Fuel Input				
Date	Quantity	Unit	Mileage	Units

Notes :

Signature :

Vehicle Mileage Logbook

Sheet no.:

Make :   Model :   Year :   License number :

DATE	PURPOSE OF TRAVEL	JOURNEY		ODOMETER READING			TOTAL MILES	
		From	To	Start	End	Distance (km)	Business	Private

Daily checks	Tires/ Wheel	Wipers	Lights	Mirrors	Horn	Seatbelts	Brakes	Coupling devices
Monday								
Tuesday								
Wednesday								
Thursday								
Friday								
Saturday								
Sunday								

Fuel Input				
Date	Quantity	Unit	Mileage	Units

Notes :

_____
_____
_____
_____
_____
_____
_____

Signature :

Vehicle Mileage Logbook

Sheet no.:

Make :   Model :   Year :   License number :

DATE	PURPOSE OF TRAVEL	JOURNEY		ODOMETER READING			TOTAL MILES	
		From	To	Start	End	Distance (km)	Business	Private

Daily checks	Tires/ Wheel	Wipers	Lights	Mirrors	Horn	Seatbelts	Brakes	Coupling devices
Monday								
Tuesday								
Wednesday								
Thursday								
Friday								
Saturday								
Sunday								

Fuel Input				
Date	Quantity	Unit	Mileage	Units

Notes :

_____
_____
_____
_____
_____
_____
_____
_____

Signature :

Vehicle Mileage Logbook

Sheet no.:

Make :		Model :		Year :	License number :

DATE	PURPOSE OF TRAVEL	JOURNEY		ODOMETER READING			TOTAL MILES	
		From	To	Start	End	Distance (km)	Business	Private

Daily checks	Tires/ Wheel	Wipers	Lights	Mirrors	Horn	Seatbelts	Brakes	Coupling devices
Monday								
Tuesday								
Wednesday								
Thursday								
Friday								
Saturday								
Sunday								

Fuel Input				
Date	Quantity	Unit	Mileage	Units

Notes :

_____
_____
_____
_____
_____
_____
_____
_____

Signature :

Vehicle Mileage Logbook

	Sheet no.:

Make :   Model :   Year :   License number :

DATE	PURPOSE OF TRAVEL	JOURNEY		ODOMETER READING			TOTAL MILES	
		From	To	Start	End	Distance (km)	Business	Private

Daily checks	Tires/ Wheel	Wipers	Lights	Mirrors	Horn	Seatbelts	Brakes	Coupling devices
Monday								
Tuesday								
Wednesday								
Thursday								
Friday								
Saturday								
Sunday								

Fuel Input				
Date	Quantity	Unit	Mileage	Units

Notes :

_____
_____
_____
_____
_____
_____
_____
_____

Signature :

Vehicle Mileage Logbook

Sheet no.:

Make :　　　　Model :　　　　Year :　　License number :

DATE	PURPOSE OF TRAVEL	JOURNEY		ODOMETER READING			TOTAL MILES	
		From	To	Start	End	Distance (km)	Business	Private

Daily checks	Tires/ Wheel	Wipers	Lights	Mirrors	Horn	Seatbelts	Brakes	Coupling devices
Monday								
Tuesday								
Wednesday								
Thursday								
Friday								
Saturday								
Sunday								

Fuel Input				
Date	Quantity	Unit	Mileage	Units

Notes :

_____
_____
_____
_____
_____
_____
_____
_____

Signature :

Vehicle Mileage Logbook

Sheet no.:

Make :		Model :			Year :		License number :	

DATE	PURPOSE OF TRAVEL	JOURNEY		ODOMETER READING			TOTAL MILES	
		From	To	Start	End	Distance (km)	Business	Private

Daily checks	Tires/ Wheel	Wipers	Lights	Mirrors	Horn	Seatbelts	Brakes	Coupling devices
Monday								
Tuesday								
Wednesday								
Thursday								
Friday								
Saturday								
Sunday								

Fuel Input				
Date	Quantity	Unit	Mileage	Units

Notes :

Signature :

Vehicle Mileage Logbook

Sheet no.:

Make :   Model :   Year :   License number :

DATE	PURPOSE OF TRAVEL	JOURNEY		ODOMETER READING			TOTAL MILES	
		From	To	Start	End	Distance (km)	Business	Private

Daily checks	Tires/ Wheel	Wipers	Lights	Mirrors	Horn	Seatbelts	Brakes	Coupling devices
Monday								
Tuesday								
Wednesday								
Thursday								
Friday								
Saturday								
Sunday								

Fuel Input				
Date	Quantity	Unit	Mileage	Units

Notes :

Signature :

Vehicle Mileage Logbook

Sheet no.:

Make :   Model :   Year :   License number :

DATE	PURPOSE OF TRAVEL	JOURNEY		ODOMETER READING			TOTAL MILES	
		From	To	Start	End	Distance (km)	Business	Private

Daily checks	Tires/ Wheel	Wipers	Lights	Mirrors	Horn	Seatbelts	Brakes	Coupling devices
Monday								
Tuesday								
Wednesday								
Thursday								
Friday								
Saturday								
Sunday								

Fuel Input				
Date	Quantity	Unit	Mileage	Units

Notes :

_____
_____
_____
_____
_____
_____
_____

Signature :

Vehicle Mileage Logbook

Sheet no.:

Make :　　　　Model :　　　　Year :　　　License number :

DATE	PURPOSE OF TRAVEL	JOURNEY		ODOMETER READING			TOTAL MILES	
		From	To	Start	End	Distance (km)	Business	Private

Daily checks	Tires/ Wheel	Wipers	Lights	Mirrors	Horn	Seatbelts	Brakes	Coupling devices
Monday								
Tuesday								
Wednesday								
Thursday								
Friday								
Saturday								
Sunday								

Fuel Input				
Date	Quantity	Unit	Mileage	Units

Notes :

Signature :

Vehicle Mileage Logbook

Sheet no.:

Make :   Model :   Year :   License number :

| DATE | PURPOSE OF TRAVEL | JOURNEY | | ODOMETER READING | | | TOTAL MILES | |
		From	To	Start	End	Distance (km)	Business	Private

Daily checks	Tires/ Wheel	Wipers	Lights	Mirrors	Horn	Seatbelts	Brakes	Coupling devices
Monday								
Tuesday								
Wednesday								
Thursday								
Friday								
Saturday								
Sunday								

| Fuel Input | | | | |
Date	Quantity	Unit	Mileage	Units

Notes :

_____
_____
_____
_____
_____
_____
_____

Signature :

Vehicle Mileage Logbook

Sheet no.:

Make :	Model :	Year :	License number :

DATE	PURPOSE OF TRAVEL	JOURNEY		ODOMETER READING			TOTAL MILES	
		From	To	Start	End	Distance (km)	Business	Private

Daily checks	Tires/ Wheel	Wipers	Lights	Mirrors	Horn	Seatbelts	Brakes	Coupling devices
Monday								
Tuesday								
Wednesday								
Thursday								
Friday								
Saturday								
Sunday								

Fuel Input				
Date	Quantity	Unit	Mileage	Units

Notes :

Signature :

Vehicle Mileage Logbook

Sheet no.:

Make :　　　　Model :　　　　Year :　　　License number :

DATE	PURPOSE OF TRAVEL	JOURNEY		ODOMETER READING			TOTAL MILES	
		From	To	Start	End	Distance (km)	Business	Private

Daily checks	Tires/ Wheel	Wipers	Lights	Mirrors	Horn	Seatbelts	Brakes	Coupling devices
Monday								
Tuesday								
Wednesday								
Thursday								
Friday								
Saturday								
Sunday								

Fuel Input				
Date	Quantity	Unit	Mileage	Units

Notes :

Signature :

Vehicle Mileage Logbook

Sheet no.:

Make :　　　　Model :　　　　Year :　　　License number :

DATE	PURPOSE OF TRAVEL	JOURNEY		ODOMETER READING			TOTAL MILES	
		From	To	Start	End	Distance (km)	Business	Private

Daily checks	Tires/ Wheel	Wipers	Lights	Mirrors	Horn	Seatbelts	Brakes	Coupling devices
Monday								
Tuesday								
Wednesday								
Thursday								
Friday								
Saturday								
Sunday								

Fuel Input				
Date	Quantity	Unit	Mileage	Units

Notes :

_____
_____
_____
_____
_____
_____
_____
_____

Signature :

Vehicle Mileage Logbook

Sheet no.:

Make :   Model :   Year :   License number :

DATE	PURPOSE OF TRAVEL	JOURNEY		ODOMETER READING			TOTAL MILES	
		From	To	Start	End	Distance (km)	Business	Private

Daily checks	Tires/ Wheel	Wipers	Lights	Mirrors	Horn	Seatbelts	Brakes	Coupling devices
Monday								
Tuesday								
Wednesday								
Thursday								
Friday								
Saturday								
Sunday								

Fuel Input				
Date	Quantity	Unit	Mileage	Units

Notes :

Signature :

Vehicle Mileage Logbook

Sheet no.:

Make :   Model :   Year :   License number :

DATE	PURPOSE OF TRAVEL	JOURNEY		ODOMETER READING			TOTAL MILES	
		From	To	Start	End	Distance (km)	Business	Private

Daily checks	Tires/ Wheel	Wipers	Lights	Mirrors	Horn	Seatbelts	Brakes	Coupling devices
Monday								
Tuesday								
Wednesday								
Thursday								
Friday								
Saturday								
Sunday								

Fuel Input				
Date	Quantity	Unit	Mileage	Units

Notes :

Signature :

Vehicle Mileage Logbook

Sheet no.:

Make :   Model :   Year :   License number :

DATE	PURPOSE OF TRAVEL	JOURNEY		ODOMETER READING			TOTAL MILES	
		From	To	Start	End	Distance (km)	Business	Private

Daily checks	Tires/ Wheel	Wipers	Lights	Mirrors	Horn	Seatbelts	Brakes	Coupling devices
Monday								
Tuesday								
Wednesday								
Thursday								
Friday								
Saturday								
Sunday								

Fuel Input				
Date	Quantity	Unit	Mileage	Units

Notes :

Signature :

Vehicle Mileage Logbook

Sheet no.:

Make :   Model :   Year :   License number :

DATE	PURPOSE OF TRAVEL	JOURNEY		ODOMETER READING			TOTAL MILES	
		From	To	Start	End	Distance (km)	Business	Private

Daily checks	Tires/ Wheel	Wipers	Lights	Mirrors	Horn	Seatbelts	Brakes	Coupling devices
Monday								
Tuesday								
Wednesday								
Thursday								
Friday								
Saturday								
Sunday								

Fuel Input				
Date	Quantity	Unit	Mileage	Units

Notes :

Signature :

Vehicle Mileage Logbook

Sheet no.:

Make :   Model :   Year :   License number :

DATE	PURPOSE OF TRAVEL	JOURNEY		ODOMETER READING			TOTAL MILES	
		From	To	Start	End	Distance (km)	Business	Private

Daily checks	Tires/ Wheel	Wipers	Lights	Mirrors	Horn	Seatbelts	Brakes	Coupling devices
Monday								
Tuesday								
Wednesday								
Thursday								
Friday								
Saturday								
Sunday								

Fuel Input				
Date	Quantity	Unit	Mileage	Units

Notes :

_____
_____
_____
_____
_____
_____
_____
_____

Signature :

Vehicle Mileage Logbook

Sheet no.:

Make :　　　　Model :　　　　Year :　　License number :

DATE	PURPOSE OF TRAVEL	JOURNEY		ODOMETER READING			TOTAL MILES	
		From	To	Start	End	Distance (km)	Business	Private

Daily checks	Tires/ Wheel	Wipers	Lights	Mirrors	Horn	Seatbelts	Brakes	Coupling devices
Monday								
Tuesday								
Wednesday								
Thursday								
Friday								
Saturday								
Sunday								

Fuel Input				
Date	Quantity	Unit	Mileage	Units

Notes :

Signature :

Vehicle Mileage Logbook

Sheet no.:

Make :   Model :   Year :   License number :

DATE	PURPOSE OF TRAVEL	JOURNEY		ODOMETER READING			TOTAL MILES	
		From	To	Start	End	Distance (km)	Business	Private

Daily checks	Tires/ Wheel	Wipers	Lights	Mirrors	Horn	Seatbelts	Brakes	Coupling devices
Monday								
Tuesday								
Wednesday								
Thursday								
Friday								
Saturday								
Sunday								

Fuel Input				
Date	Quantity	Unit	Mileage	Units

Notes :

_____
_____
_____
_____
_____
_____
_____
_____

Signature :

Vehicle Mileage Logbook

Sheet no.:

Make :   Model :   Year :   License number :

DATE	PURPOSE OF TRAVEL	JOURNEY		ODOMETER READING			TOTAL MILES	
		From	To	Start	End	Distance (km)	Business	Private

Daily checks	Tires/ Wheel	Wipers	Lights	Mirrors	Horn	Seatbelts	Brakes	Coupling devices
Monday								
Tuesday								
Wednesday								
Thursday								
Friday								
Saturday								
Sunday								

Fuel Input				
Date	Quantity	Unit	Mileage	Units

Notes :

_____
_____
_____
_____
_____
_____
_____
_____

Signature :

Vehicle Mileage Logbook

Sheet no.:

Make :   Model :   Year :   License number :

DATE	PURPOSE OF TRAVEL	JOURNEY		ODOMETER READING			TOTAL MILES	
		From	To	Start	End	Distance (km)	Business	Private

Daily checks	Tires/ Wheel	Wipers	Lights	Mirrors	Horn	Seatbelts	Brakes	Coupling devices
Monday								
Tuesday								
Wednesday								
Thursday								
Friday								
Saturday								
Sunday								

Fuel Input				
Date	Quantity	Unit	Mileage	Units

Notes :

_____
_____
_____
_____
_____
_____
_____

Signature :

Vehicle Mileage Logbook

			Sheet no.:
Make :	Model :	Year :	License number :

DATE	PURPOSE OF TRAVEL	JOURNEY		ODOMETER READING			TOTAL MILES	
		From	To	Start	End	Distance (km)	Business	Private

Daily checks	Tires/ Wheel	Wipers	Lights	Mirrors	Horn	Seatbelts	Brakes	Coupling devices
Monday								
Tuesday								
Wednesday								
Thursday								
Friday								
Saturday								
Sunday								

Fuel Input				
Date	Quantity	Unit	Mileage	Units

Notes :

_____

_____

_____

_____

_____

_____

_____

Signature :

Vehicle Mileage Logbook

Sheet no.:

Make :   Model :   Year :   License number :

DATE	PURPOSE OF TRAVEL	JOURNEY		ODOMETER READING			TOTAL MILES	
		From	To	Start	End	Distance (km)	Business	Private

Daily checks	Tires/ Wheel	Wipers	Lights	Mirrors	Horn	Seatbelts	Brakes	Coupling devices
Monday								
Tuesday								
Wednesday								
Thursday								
Friday								
Saturday								
Sunday								

Fuel Input				
Date	Quantity	Unit	Mileage	Units

Notes :

Signature :

Vehicle Mileage Logbook

Sheet no.:

Make :　　　　Model :　　　　Year :　　　License number :

DATE	PURPOSE OF TRAVEL	JOURNEY		ODOMETER READING			TOTAL MILES	
		From	To	Start	End	Distance (km)	Business	Private

Daily checks	Tires/ Wheel	Wipers	Lights	Mirrors	Horn	Seatbelts	Brakes	Coupling devices
Monday								
Tuesday								
Wednesday								
Thursday								
Friday								
Saturday								
Sunday								

Fuel Input				
Date	Quantity	Unit	Mileage	Units

Notes :

_____
_____
_____
_____
_____
_____
_____

Signature :

Vehicle Mileage Logbook

Sheet no.:

Make : Model : Year : License number :

DATE	PURPOSE OF TRAVEL	JOURNEY		ODOMETER READING			TOTAL MILES	
		From	To	Start	End	Distance (km)	Business	Private

Daily checks	Tires/ Wheel	Wipers	Lights	Mirrors	Horn	Seatbelts	Brakes	Coupling devices
Monday								
Tuesday								
Wednesday								
Thursday								
Friday								
Saturday								
Sunday								

Fuel Input				
Date	Quantity	Unit	Mileage	Units

Notes :

Signature :

Vehicle Mileage Logbook

Sheet no.:

Make :　　　　　　Model :　　　　　　　　　Year :　　　License number :

DATE	PURPOSE OF TRAVEL	JOURNEY		ODOMETER READING			TOTAL MILES	
		From	To	Start	End	Distance (km)	Business	Private

Daily checks	Tires/ Wheel	Wipers	Lights	Mirrors	Horn	Seatbelts	Brakes	Coupling devices
Monday								
Tuesday								
Wednesday								
Thursday								
Friday								
Saturday								
Sunday								

Fuel Input				
Date	Quantity	Unit	Mileage	Units

Notes :

_____
_____
_____
_____
_____
_____
_____
_____

Signature :

Vehicle Mileage Logbook

Sheet no.:

Make :   Model :   Year :   License number :

DATE	PURPOSE OF TRAVEL	JOURNEY		ODOMETER READING			TOTAL MILES	
		From	To	Start	End	Distance (km)	Business	Private

Daily checks	Tires/ Wheel	Wipers	Lights	Mirrors	Horn	Seatbelts	Brakes	Coupling devices
Monday								
Tuesday								
Wednesday								
Thursday								
Friday								
Saturday								
Sunday								

Fuel Input				
Date	Quantity	Unit	Mileage	Units

Notes :

Signature :

Vehicle Mileage Logbook

Sheet no.:

Make :   Model :   Year :   License number :

DATE	PURPOSE OF TRAVEL	JOURNEY		ODOMETER READING			TOTAL MILES	
		From	To	Start	End	Distance (km)	Business	Private

Daily checks	Tires/ Wheel	Wipers	Lights	Mirrors	Horn	Seatbelts	Brakes	Coupling devices
Monday								
Tuesday								
Wednesday								
Thursday								
Friday								
Saturday								
Sunday								

Fuel Input				
Date	Quantity	Unit	Mileage	Units

Notes :

_____
_____
_____
_____
_____
_____
_____
_____

Signature :

Vehicle Mileage Logbook

Sheet no.:

Make :　　　Model :　　　Year :　　　License number :

DATE	PURPOSE OF TRAVEL	JOURNEY		ODOMETER READING			TOTAL MILES	
		From	To	Start	End	Distance (km)	Business	Private

Daily checks	Tires/ Wheel	Wipers	Lights	Mirrors	Horn	Seatbelts	Brakes	Coupling devices
Monday								
Tuesday								
Wednesday								
Thursday								
Friday								
Saturday								
Sunday								

Fuel Input				
Date	Quantity	Unit	Mileage	Units

Notes :

Signature :

Vehicle Mileage Logbook

Sheet no.:

Make :   **Model :**   **Year :**   **License number :**

DATE	PURPOSE OF TRAVEL	JOURNEY		ODOMETER READING			TOTAL MILES	
		From	To	Start	End	Distance (km)	Business	Private

Daily checks	Tires/ Wheel	Wipers	Lights	Mirrors	Horn	Seatbelts	Brakes	Coupling devices
Monday								
Tuesday								
Wednesday								
Thursday								
Friday								
Saturday								
Sunday								

Fuel Input				
Date	Quantity	Unit	Mileage	Units

Notes :

Signature :

Vehicle Mileage Logbook

Sheet no.:

Make :　　　　Model :　　　　Year :　　　License number :

DATE	PURPOSE OF TRAVEL	JOURNEY		ODOMETER READING			TOTAL MILES	
		From	To	Start	End	Distance (km)	Business	Private

Daily checks	Tires/ Wheel	Wipers	Lights	Mirrors	Horn	Seatbelts	Brakes	Coupling devices
Monday								
Tuesday								
Wednesday								
Thursday								
Friday								
Saturday								
Sunday								

Fuel Input				
Date	Quantity	Unit	Mileage	Units

Notes :

_____
_____
_____
_____
_____
_____
_____

Signature :

Vehicle Mileage Logbook

Sheet no.:

Make :   Model :   Year :   License number :

DATE	PURPOSE OF TRAVEL	JOURNEY		ODOMETER READING			TOTAL MILES	
		From	To	Start	End	Distance (km)	Business	Private

Daily checks	Tires/ Wheel	Wipers	Lights	Mirrors	Horn	Seatbelts	Brakes	Coupling devices
Monday								
Tuesday								
Wednesday								
Thursday								
Friday								
Saturday								
Sunday								

Fuel Input				
Date	Quantity	Unit	Mileage	Units

Notes :

Signature :

Vehicle Mileage Logbook

Sheet no.:

Make :　　　Model :　　　Year :　　　License number :

DATE	PURPOSE OF TRAVEL	JOURNEY		ODOMETER READING			TOTAL MILES	
		From	To	Start	End	Distance (km)	Business	Private

Daily checks	Tires/ Wheel	Wipers	Lights	Mirrors	Horn	Seatbelts	Brakes	Coupling devices
Monday								
Tuesday								
Wednesday								
Thursday								
Friday								
Saturday								
Sunday								

Fuel Input				
Date	Quantity	Unit	Mileage	Units

Notes :

Signature :

Vehicle Mileage Logbook

Sheet no.:

Make : | **Model :** | **Year :** | **License number :**

DATE	PURPOSE OF TRAVEL	JOURNEY		ODOMETER READING			TOTAL MILES	
		From	To	Start	End	Distance (km)	Business	Private

Daily checks	Tires/ Wheel	Wipers	Lights	Mirrors	Horn	Seatbelts	Brakes	Coupling devices
Monday								
Tuesday								
Wednesday								
Thursday								
Friday								
Saturday								
Sunday								

Fuel Input				
Date	Quantity	Unit	Mileage	Units

Notes :

_____
_____
_____
_____
_____
_____
_____
_____

Signature :

Vehicle Mileage Logbook

Sheet no.:

Make : Model : Year : License number :

DATE	PURPOSE OF TRAVEL	JOURNEY		ODOMETER READING			TOTAL MILES	
		From	To	Start	End	Distance (km)	Business	Private

Daily checks	Tires/ Wheel	Wipers	Lights	Mirrors	Horn	Seatbelts	Brakes	Coupling devices
Monday								
Tuesday								
Wednesday								
Thursday								
Friday								
Saturday								
Sunday								

Fuel Input				
Date	Quantity	Unit	Mileage	Units

Notes :

Signature :

Vehicle Mileage Logbook

Sheet no.:

Make :   Model :   Year :   License number :

DATE	PURPOSE OF TRAVEL	JOURNEY		ODOMETER READING			TOTAL MILES	
		From	To	Start	End	Distance (km)	Business	Private

Daily checks	Tires/ Wheel	Wipers	Lights	Mirrors	Horn	Seatbelts	Brakes	Coupling devices
Monday								
Tuesday								
Wednesday								
Thursday								
Friday								
Saturday								
Sunday								

Fuel Input				
Date	Quantity	Unit	Mileage	Units

Notes :

Signature :

Vehicle Mileage Logbook

Sheet no.:

| Make : | | Model : | | Year : | | License number : | |

DATE	PURPOSE OF TRAVEL	JOURNEY		ODOMETER READING			TOTAL MILES	
		From	To	Start	End	Distance (km)	Business	Private

Daily checks	Tires/ Wheel	Wipers	Lights	Mirrors	Horn	Seatbelts	Brakes	Coupling devices
Monday								
Tuesday								
Wednesday								
Thursday								
Friday								
Saturday								
Sunday								

Fuel Input				
Date	Quantity	Unit	Mileage	Units

Notes :

Signature :

Vehicle Mileage Logbook

Sheet no.:

Make :   Model :   Year :   License number :

DATE	PURPOSE OF TRAVEL	JOURNEY		ODOMETER READING			TOTAL MILES	
		From	To	Start	End	Distance (km)	Business	Private

Daily checks	Tires/ Wheel	Wipers	Lights	Mirrors	Horn	Seatbelts	Brakes	Coupling devices
Monday								
Tuesday								
Wednesday								
Thursday								
Friday								
Saturday								
Sunday								

Fuel Input				
Date	Quantity	Unit	Mileage	Units

Notes :

_____
_____
_____
_____
_____
_____
_____
_____

Signature :

Vehicle Mileage Logbook

Sheet no.:

Make :   Model :   Year :   License number :

DATE	PURPOSE OF TRAVEL	JOURNEY		ODOMETER READING			TOTAL MILES	
		From	To	Start	End	Distance (km)	Business	Private

Daily checks	Tires/ Wheel	Wipers	Lights	Mirrors	Horn	Seatbelts	Brakes	Coupling devices
Monday								
Tuesday								
Wednesday								
Thursday								
Friday								
Saturday								
Sunday								

Fuel Input				
Date	Quantity	Unit	Mileage	Units

Notes :

_____
_____
_____
_____
_____
_____
_____
_____

Signature :

Vehicle Mileage Logbook

Sheet no.:

Make :   Model :   Year :   License number :

DATE	PURPOSE OF TRAVEL	JOURNEY		ODOMETER READING			TOTAL MILES	
		From	To	Start	End	Distance (km)	Business	Private

Daily checks	Tires/ Wheel	Wipers	Lights	Mirrors	Horn	Seatbelts	Brakes	Coupling devices
Monday								
Tuesday								
Wednesday								
Thursday								
Friday								
Saturday								
Sunday								

Fuel Input				
Date	Quantity	Unit	Mileage	Units

Notes :

_____

_____

_____

_____

_____

_____

_____

Signature :

Vehicle Mileage Logbook

Sheet no.:

Make :   Model :   Year :   License number :

DATE	PURPOSE OF TRAVEL	JOURNEY		ODOMETER READING			TOTAL MILES	
		From	To	Start	End	Distance (km)	Business	Private

Daily checks	Tires/ Wheel	Wipers	Lights	Mirrors	Horn	Seatbelts	Brakes	Coupling devices
Monday								
Tuesday								
Wednesday								
Thursday								
Friday								
Saturday								
Sunday								

Fuel Input				
Date	Quantity	Unit	Mileage	Units

Notes :
_____
_____
_____
_____
_____
_____
_____
_____

Signature :

Vehicle Mileage Logbook

Sheet no.:

Make :   Model :   Year :   License number :

DATE	PURPOSE OF TRAVEL	JOURNEY		ODOMETER READING			TOTAL MILES	
		From	To	Start	End	Distance (km)	Business	Private

Daily checks	Tires/ Wheel	Wipers	Lights	Mirrors	Horn	Seatbelts	Brakes	Coupling devices
Monday								
Tuesday								
Wednesday								
Thursday								
Friday								
Saturday								
Sunday								

Fuel Input				
Date	Quantity	Unit	Mileage	Units

Notes :

_____
_____
_____
_____
_____
_____
_____
_____

Signature :

Vehicle Mileage Logbook

Sheet no.:

Make :		Model :		Year :		License number :

DATE	PURPOSE OF TRAVEL	JOURNEY		ODOMETER READING			TOTAL MILES	
		From	To	Start	End	Distance (km)	Business	Private

Daily checks	Tires/ Wheel	Wipers	Lights	Mirrors	Horn	Seatbelts	Brakes	Coupling devices
Monday								
Tuesday								
Wednesday								
Thursday								
Friday								
Saturday								
Sunday								

Fuel Input					Notes :
Date	Quantity	Unit	Mileage	Units	
					Signature :

Vehicle Mileage Logbook

Sheet no.:

Make :　　　　Model :　　　　Year :　　　License number :

DATE	PURPOSE OF TRAVEL	JOURNEY		ODOMETER READING			TOTAL MILES	
		From	To	Start	End	Distance (km)	Business	Private

Daily checks	Tires/ Wheel	Wipers	Lights	Mirrors	Horn	Seatbelts	Brakes	Coupling devices
Monday								
Tuesday								
Wednesday								
Thursday								
Friday								
Saturday								
Sunday								

Fuel Input				
Date	Quantity	Unit	Mileage	Units

Notes :

_____

_____

_____

_____

_____

_____

_____

Signature :

Vehicle Mileage Logbook

Sheet no.:

Make :　　　　　Model :　　　　　Year :　　　　　License number :

DATE	PURPOSE OF TRAVEL	JOURNEY		ODOMETER READING			TOTAL MILES	
		From	To	Start	End	Distance (km)	Business	Private

Daily checks	Tires/ Wheel	Wipers	Lights	Mirrors	Horn	Seatbelts	Brakes	Coupling devices
Monday								
Tuesday								
Wednesday								
Thursday								
Friday								
Saturday								
Sunday								

Fuel Input				
Date	Quantity	Unit	Mileage	Units

Notes :

_____
_____
_____
_____
_____
_____
_____
_____
_____

Signature :

Vehicle Mileage Logbook

Sheet no.:

Make : Model : Year : License number :

DATE	PURPOSE OF TRAVEL	JOURNEY		ODOMETER READING			TOTAL MILES	
		From	To	Start	End	Distance (km)	Business	Private

Daily checks	Tires/ Wheel	Wipers	Lights	Mirrors	Horn	Seatbelts	Brakes	Coupling devices
Monday								
Tuesday								
Wednesday								
Thursday								
Friday								
Saturday								
Sunday								

Fuel Input				
Date	Quantity	Unit	Mileage	Units

Notes :

Signature :

Vehicle Mileage Logbook

Sheet no.:

Make :   Model :   Year :   License number :

DATE	PURPOSE OF TRAVEL	JOURNEY		ODOMETER READING			TOTAL MILES	
		From	To	Start	End	Distance (km)	Business	Private

Daily checks	Tires/ Wheel	Wipers	Lights	Mirrors	Horn	Seatbelts	Brakes	Coupling devices
Monday								
Tuesday								
Wednesday								
Thursday								
Friday								
Saturday								
Sunday								

Fuel Input				
Date	Quantity	Unit	Mileage	Units

Notes :

_____
_____
_____
_____
_____
_____
_____
_____

Signature :

Vehicle Mileage Logbook

Sheet no.:

Make :　　　　Model :　　　　Year :　　　　License number :

DATE	PURPOSE OF TRAVEL	JOURNEY		ODOMETER READING			TOTAL MILES	
		From	To	Start	End	Distance (km)	Business	Private

Daily checks	Tires/ Wheel	Wipers	Lights	Mirrors	Horn	Seatbelts	Brakes	Coupling devices
Monday								
Tuesday								
Wednesday								
Thursday								
Friday								
Saturday								
Sunday								

Fuel Input				
Date	Quantity	Unit	Mileage	Units

Notes :

_____
_____
_____
_____
_____
_____
_____
_____

Signature :

Vehicle Mileage Logbook

Sheet no.:

Make : Model : Year : License number :

DATE	PURPOSE OF TRAVEL	JOURNEY		ODOMETER READING			TOTAL MILES	
		From	To	Start	End	Distance (km)	Business	Private

Daily checks	Tires/ Wheel	Wipers	Lights	Mirrors	Horn	Seatbelts	Brakes	Coupling devices
Monday								
Tuesday								
Wednesday								
Thursday								
Friday								
Saturday								
Sunday								

Fuel Input				
Date	Quantity	Unit	Mileage	Units

Notes :

Signature :

Vehicle Mileage Logbook

Sheet no.:

Make :   Model :   Year :   License number :

DATE	PURPOSE OF TRAVEL	JOURNEY		ODOMETER READING			TOTAL MILES	
		From	To	Start	End	Distance (km)	Business	Private

Daily checks	Tires/ Wheel	Wipers	Lights	Mirrors	Horn	Seatbelts	Brakes	Coupling devices
Monday								
Tuesday								
Wednesday								
Thursday								
Friday								
Saturday								
Sunday								

Fuel Input				
Date	Quantity	Unit	Mileage	Units

Notes :

_____
_____
_____
_____
_____
_____
_____
_____

Signature :

Vehicle Mileage Logbook

Sheet no.:

Make :   Model :   Year :   License number :

DATE	PURPOSE OF TRAVEL	JOURNEY		ODOMETER READING			TOTAL MILES	
		From	To	Start	End	Distance (km)	Business	Private

Daily checks	Tires/ Wheel	Wipers	Lights	Mirrors	Horn	Seatbelts	Brakes	Coupling devices
Monday								
Tuesday								
Wednesday								
Thursday								
Friday								
Saturday								
Sunday								

Fuel Input				
Date	Quantity	Unit	Mileage	Units

Notes :

Signature :

Vehicle Mileage Logbook

Sheet no.:

Make :　　　　Model :　　　　Year :　　License number :

DATE	PURPOSE OF TRAVEL	JOURNEY		ODOMETER READING			TOTAL MILES	
		From	To	Start	End	Distance (km)	Business	Private

Daily checks	Tires/ Wheel	Wipers	Lights	Mirrors	Horn	Seatbelts	Brakes	Coupling devices
Monday								
Tuesday								
Wednesday								
Thursday								
Friday								
Saturday								
Sunday								

Fuel Input				
Date	Quantity	Unit	Mileage	Units

Notes :

_____
_____
_____
_____
_____
_____
_____

Signature :

Vehicle Mileage Logbook

Sheet no.:

Make :   Model :   Year :   License number :

DATE	PURPOSE OF TRAVEL	JOURNEY		ODOMETER READING			TOTAL MILES	
		From	To	Start	End	Distance (km)	Business	Private

Daily checks	Tires/ Wheel	Wipers	Lights	Mirrors	Horn	Seatbelts	Brakes	Coupling devices
Monday								
Tuesday								
Wednesday								
Thursday								
Friday								
Saturday								
Sunday								

Fuel Input				
Date	Quantity	Unit	Mileage	Units

Notes :

Signature :

Vehicle Mileage Logbook

	Sheet no.:

Make :	Model :	Year :	License number :

DATE	PURPOSE OF TRAVEL	JOURNEY		ODOMETER READING			TOTAL MILES	
		From	To	Start	End	Distance (km)	Business	Private

Daily checks	Tires/ Wheel	Wipers	Lights	Mirrors	Horn	Seatbelts	Brakes	Coupling devices
Monday								
Tuesday								
Wednesday								
Thursday								
Friday								
Saturday								
Sunday								

Fuel Input				
Date	Quantity	Unit	Mileage	Units

Notes :

_____
_____
_____
_____
_____
_____
_____
_____

Signature :

Vehicle Mileage Logbook

Sheet no.:

Make :   Model :   Year :   License number :

DATE	PURPOSE OF TRAVEL	JOURNEY		ODOMETER READING			TOTAL MILES	
		From	To	Start	End	Distance (km)	Business	Private

Daily checks	Tires/ Wheel	Wipers	Lights	Mirrors	Horn	Seatbelts	Brakes	Coupling devices
Monday								
Tuesday								
Wednesday								
Thursday								
Friday								
Saturday								
Sunday								

Fuel Input				
Date	Quantity	Unit	Mileage	Units

Notes :

Signature :

Vehicle Mileage Logbook

Sheet no.:

Make :　　　　Model :　　　　Year :　　　　License number :

DATE	PURPOSE OF TRAVEL	JOURNEY		ODOMETER READING			TOTAL MILES	
		From	To	Start	End	Distance (km)	Business	Private

Daily checks	Tires/ Wheel	Wipers	Lights	Mirrors	Horn	Seatbelts	Brakes	Coupling devices
Monday								
Tuesday								
Wednesday								
Thursday								
Friday								
Saturday								
Sunday								

Fuel Input				
Date	Quantity	Unit	Mileage	Units

Notes :

Signature :

Vehicle Mileage Logbook

Sheet no.:

Make :　　　　　Model :　　　　　Year :　　　　License number :

DATE	PURPOSE OF TRAVEL	JOURNEY		ODOMETER READING			TOTAL MILES	
		From	To	Start	End	Distance (km)	Business	Private

Daily checks	Tires/ Wheel	Wipers	Lights	Mirrors	Horn	Seatbelts	Brakes	Coupling devices
Monday								
Tuesday								
Wednesday								
Thursday								
Friday								
Saturday								
Sunday								

Fuel Input				
Date	Quantity	Unit	Mileage	Units

Notes :

Signature :

Vehicle Mileage Logbook

Sheet no.:

Make :　　　　Model :　　　　Year :　　　　License number :

DATE	PURPOSE OF TRAVEL	JOURNEY		ODOMETER READING			TOTAL MILES	
		From	To	Start	End	Distance (km)	Business	Private

Daily checks	Tires/ Wheel	Wipers	Lights	Mirrors	Horn	Seatbelts	Brakes	Coupling devices
Monday								
Tuesday								
Wednesday								
Thursday								
Friday								
Saturday								
Sunday								

Fuel Input				
Date	Quantity	Unit	Mileage	Units

Notes :

Signature :

Vehicle Mileage Logbook

Sheet no.:

Make :   Model :   Year :   License number :

DATE	PURPOSE OF TRAVEL	JOURNEY		ODOMETER READING			TOTAL MILES	
		From	To	Start	End	Distance (km)	Business	Private

Daily checks	Tires/ Wheel	Wipers	Lights	Mirrors	Horn	Seatbelts	Brakes	Coupling devices
Monday								
Tuesday								
Wednesday								
Thursday								
Friday								
Saturday								
Sunday								

Fuel Input				
Date	Quantity	Unit	Mileage	Units

Notes :

Signature :

Vehicle Mileage Logbook

Sheet no.:

Make :   Model :   Year :   License number :

DATE	PURPOSE OF TRAVEL	JOURNEY		ODOMETER READING			TOTAL MILES	
		From	To	Start	End	Distance (km)	Business	Private

Daily checks	Tires/ Wheel	Wipers	Lights	Mirrors	Horn	Seatbelts	Brakes	Coupling devices
Monday								
Tuesday								
Wednesday								
Thursday								
Friday								
Saturday								
Sunday								

Fuel Input				
Date	Quantity	Unit	Mileage	Units

Notes :

_____
_____
_____
_____
_____
_____
_____
_____

Signature :

Vehicle Mileage Logbook

Sheet no.:

Make : | Model : | Year : | License number :

DATE	PURPOSE OF TRAVEL	JOURNEY		ODOMETER READING			TOTAL MILES	
		From	To	Start	End	Distance (km)	Business	Private

Daily checks	Tires/ Wheel	Wipers	Lights	Mirrors	Horn	Seatbelts	Brakes	Coupling devices
Monday								
Tuesday								
Wednesday								
Thursday								
Friday								
Saturday								
Sunday								

Fuel Input				
Date	Quantity	Unit	Mileage	Units

Notes :

_____
_____
_____
_____
_____
_____
_____
_____

Signature :

Vehicle Mileage Logbook

Sheet no.:

Make :   Model :   Year :   License number :

DATE	PURPOSE OF TRAVEL	JOURNEY		ODOMETER READING			TOTAL MILES	
		From	To	Start	End	Distance (km)	Business	Private

Daily checks	Tires/ Wheel	Wipers	Lights	Mirrors	Horn	Seatbelts	Brakes	Coupling devices
Monday								
Tuesday								
Wednesday								
Thursday								
Friday								
Saturday								
Sunday								

Fuel Input				
Date	Quantity	Unit	Mileage	Units

Notes :

_____
_____
_____
_____
_____
_____
_____

Signature :

Vehicle Mileage Logbook

Sheet no.:

Make :   Model :   Year :   License number :

DATE	PURPOSE OF TRAVEL	JOURNEY		ODOMETER READING			TOTAL MILES	
		From	To	Start	End	Distance (km)	Business	Private

Daily checks	Tires/ Wheel	Wipers	Lights	Mirrors	Horn	Seatbelts	Brakes	Coupling devices
Monday								
Tuesday								
Wednesday								
Thursday								
Friday								
Saturday								
Sunday								

Fuel Input				
Date	Quantity	Unit	Mileage	Units

Notes :

Signature :

Vehicle Mileage Logbook

Sheet no.:

Make :   Model :   Year :   License number :

DATE	PURPOSE OF TRAVEL	JOURNEY		ODOMETER READING			TOTAL MILES	
		From	To	Start	End	Distance (km)	Business	Private

Daily checks	Tires/ Wheel	Wipers	Lights	Mirrors	Horn	Seatbelts	Brakes	Coupling devices
Monday								
Tuesday								
Wednesday								
Thursday								
Friday								
Saturday								
Sunday								

Fuel Input				
Date	Quantity	Unit	Mileage	Units

Notes :

_____

_____

_____

_____

_____

_____

_____

Signature :

Vehicle Mileage Logbook

Sheet no.:

Make :	Model :	Year :	License number :

DATE	PURPOSE OF TRAVEL	JOURNEY		ODOMETER READING			TOTAL MILES	
		From	To	Start	End	Distance (km)	Business	Private

Daily checks	Tires/ Wheel	Wipers	Lights	Mirrors	Horn	Seatbelts	Brakes	Coupling devices
Monday								
Tuesday								
Wednesday								
Thursday								
Friday								
Saturday								
Sunday								

Fuel Input				
Date	Quantity	Unit	Mileage	Units

Notes :

Signature :

Vehicle Mileage Logbook

Make :		**Model :**			**Year :**		**License number :**	

Sheet no.:

DATE	PURPOSE OF TRAVEL	JOURNEY		ODOMETER READING			TOTAL MILES	
		From	To	Start	End	Distance (km)	Business	Private

Daily checks	Tires/ Wheel	Wipers	Lights	Mirrors	Horn	Seatbelts	Brakes	Coupling devices
Monday								
Tuesday								
Wednesday								
Thursday								
Friday								
Saturday								
Sunday								

Fuel Input				
Date	Quantity	Unit	Mileage	Units

Notes :

_____
_____
_____
_____
_____
_____
_____

Signature :

Vehicle Mileage Logbook

Sheet no.:

Make :　　　　Model :　　　　　Year :　　License number :

DATE	PURPOSE OF TRAVEL	JOURNEY		ODOMETER READING			TOTAL MILES	
		From	To	Start	End	Distance (km)	Business	Private

Daily checks	Tires/ Wheel	Wipers	Lights	Mirrors	Horn	Seatbelts	Brakes	Coupling devices
Monday								
Tuesday								
Wednesday								
Thursday								
Friday								
Saturday								
Sunday								

Fuel Input				
Date	Quantity	Unit	Mileage	Units

Notes :

Signature :

Vehicle Mileage Logbook

Sheet no.:

Make :   Model :   Year :   License number :

DATE	PURPOSE OF TRAVEL	JOURNEY		ODOMETER READING			TOTAL MILES	
		From	To	Start	End	Distance (km)	Business	Private

Daily checks	Tires/ Wheel	Wipers	Lights	Mirrors	Horn	Seatbelts	Brakes	Coupling devices
Monday								
Tuesday								
Wednesday								
Thursday								
Friday								
Saturday								
Sunday								

Fuel Input				
Date	Quantity	Unit	Mileage	Units

Notes :
_____
_____
_____
_____
_____
_____

Signature :

Vehicle Mileage Logbook

Sheet no.:

Make :　　　　Model :　　　　Year :　　License number :

DATE	PURPOSE OF TRAVEL	JOURNEY		ODOMETER READING			TOTAL MILES	
		From	To	Start	End	Distance (km)	Business	Private

Daily checks	Tires/ Wheel	Wipers	Lights	Mirrors	Horn	Seatbelts	Brakes	Coupling devices
Monday								
Tuesday								
Wednesday								
Thursday								
Friday								
Saturday								
Sunday								

Fuel Input				
Date	Quantity	Unit	Mileage	Units

Notes :

_____
_____
_____
_____
_____
_____
_____

Signature :

Vehicle Mileage Logbook

Sheet no.:

Make : | Model : | Year : | License number :

DATE	PURPOSE OF TRAVEL	JOURNEY		ODOMETER READING			TOTAL MILES	
		From	To	Start	End	Distance (km)	Business	Private

Daily checks	Tires/ Wheel	Wipers	Lights	Mirrors	Horn	Seatbelts	Brakes	Coupling devices
Monday								
Tuesday								
Wednesday								
Thursday								
Friday								
Saturday								
Sunday								

Fuel Input				
Date	Quantity	Unit	Mileage	Units

Notes :

Signature :

Vehicle Mileage Logbook

Sheet no.:

Make :　　Model :　　Year :　　License number :

DATE	PURPOSE OF TRAVEL	JOURNEY		ODOMETER READING			TOTAL MILES	
		From	To	Start	End	Distance (km)	Business	Private

Daily checks	Tires/ Wheel	Wipers	Lights	Mirrors	Horn	Seatbelts	Brakes	Coupling devices
Monday								
Tuesday								
Wednesday								
Thursday								
Friday								
Saturday								
Sunday								

Fuel Input				
Date	Quantity	Unit	Mileage	Units

Notes :

_____
_____
_____
_____
_____
_____
_____

Signature :

Vehicle Mileage Logbook

Sheet no.:

Make :   Model :   Year :   License number :

DATE	PURPOSE OF TRAVEL	JOURNEY		ODOMETER READING			TOTAL MILES	
		From	To	Start	End	Distance (km)	Business	Private

Daily checks	Tires/ Wheel	Wipers	Lights	Mirrors	Horn	Seatbelts	Brakes	Coupling devices
Monday								
Tuesday								
Wednesday								
Thursday								
Friday								
Saturday								
Sunday								

Fuel Input				
Date	Quantity	Unit	Mileage	Units

Notes :

Signature :

Vehicle Mileage Logbook

Sheet no.:

Make :   Model :   Year :   License number :

DATE	PURPOSE OF TRAVEL	JOURNEY		ODOMETER READING			TOTAL MILES	
		From	To	Start	End	Distance (km)	Business	Private

Daily checks	Tires/ Wheel	Wipers	Lights	Mirrors	Horn	Seatbelts	Brakes	Coupling devices
Monday								
Tuesday								
Wednesday								
Thursday								
Friday								
Saturday								
Sunday								

Fuel Input				
Date	Quantity	Unit	Mileage	Units

Notes :

Signature :

Thank you!

WE ARE GLAD THAT YOU PURCHASED OUR
BOOK!
PLEASE LET US KNOW HOW WE CAN IMPROVE IT!
YOUR FEEDBACK IS ESSENTIAL TO US.

Contact us at:

M log'Sin@gmail.com

JUST TITLE THE EMAIL 'CREATIVE' AND WE WILL

GIVE YOU SOME EXTRA SURPRISES!

www.ingramcontent.com/pod-product-compliance
Lightning Source LLC
Chambersburg PA
CBHW081822200326
41597CB00023B/4355